The Crow, Hippocampus and the Angel

Show Me
The Mountain
Bright Meadows Below

Poems and illustrations
Pamela Blanchfield

100 poems and 70 illustrations

All poetry and illustrations

copyright Pamela Blanchfield

©Pamela Blanchfield 2022

All rights reserved.

No part of this publication may be reproduced, stored in a retrieval system, stored in a database and / or published in any form or by any means, electronic, mechanical, photocopying, recording or otherwise, without the prior written permission of the publisher.

Contact: sales@keyprints.plus.com

ISBN: 978-1-3999-2781-9

With special thanks to both
my good friend Kate O'Flynn
and sister-in-law Lynne Blanchfield
for their much-appreciated
insightful feedback and suggestions,
as well as their time and patience!

Also many thanks to John Whittlestone
and my brother John Blanchfield for their
valued knowledge and kind technical help

frontispiece illustration:
'The Crow, Hippocampus and the Angel'

Cover design Pamela Blanchfield

This collection is dedicated
with great love and profound thanks
to my dear muse
who rowed out to my island
and in searching for me
helped me find myself again.
A special kindred soul
can hold a magical link
that spans time and reason
and this has confirmed for me
that life and love
is mysterious and wonderful
as well as surprising!
How can I ever thank you?

What are my poems about?

Life, love, lust, dreams, desire, loss,
people, places, and our shadows both
in reality and what I perceive as glimpses
through the veils to beyond, or the unknown.

Sometimes in life we inevitably struggle
when faced with mountains we know we
must scale and if we ask – and maybe we
don't even have to consciously do that, just
be aware, notice, I believe that links and
signs of love come to us, giving strength,
direction and helping guide our way.

This collection came about as the result
of a personal event, or perhaps several
and is partly a journey back to a place
and time when I was a different person,
and, although that same version of me
still remains, inevitably it is one
entirely different now for the future.

We are all evolving in our transient given spaces
and this collection is a short visit to
my recent times, recollections and thoughts.

My hope is that others will find they can relate,
perhaps also find encouragement in difficulties
or just simply enjoy reading the verse.

Table of Contents

Dedication 5

What are my poems about?... 6

We Stood With the Stars... 13

The Wild Horse - *illustration* 14

Shadow Times 16

Trod These Paths - *illustration* 18

The Keys - *illustration* 20

Forest Hollows - *illustration* 22

Hidden Lives 24

All the Times.. 25

Two Lives - *illustration*.. 26

The Magic - *illustration*... 28

The Crow, Hippocampus and the Angel - *illustration* ... 30

Threads Still Run - *illustration* 32

Venus and Mars - *illustration* 34

Reflection 36

Facets 37

Let the Dryads Play.. 38

A Hidden Husk - *illustration*....................................... 39

Fiery Fate... 40

Looking Longer Back - *illustration* 42

Still in my Mind - *illustration* 44

A Silent Street - *illustration* 47

Summer Song - *illustration* 48

That Young Guy 50

Young Bird - *illustration* 52

Another Moon - *illustration* 55

Our Days - *illustration* 56

The Phoenix - *illustration* 58

Watch the Tides - *illustration* 60

A Wish For You - *illustration* 62

The Wild Place - *illustration* 64

Doubt You Ever Knew - *illustration* 66

Will You Take A Walk - *illustration* 69

My Lost Way 70

November Dreams - *illustration* 71

Spider Spins a Web 72

At the Crossroads - *illustration* 74

Priestess - *illustration* 76

The Other Ones - *illustration* 78

That Dublin Evening... 80

Seagulls Scream 82

The Truth - *illustration* 84

The Fourth One - *illustration* 86

The Scale - *illustration* 88

Silent Fight - *illustration* 90

Crows Early Call 91

Dormant 92

Wish With Me - *illustration* 93

Remember - *illustration* 94

Catch the Water - *illustration* 96

Fasten Those Bars Tight 98

Perfume of Roses - *illustration* 100

World of Words - *illustration* 101

Calling To Somewhere - *illustration* 102

Fool 104

I Know 105

Future Days - *illustration* 106

One Way Street - *illustration* 108

Love Remains - *illustration* 110

Just Some Yesterday - *illustration* 112

Disease 114

The Luck 116

In the Desert - *illustration* 118

Glances 121

Baby Dawn - *illustration* 122

New Red Sunrise - *illustration* 124

If You Think - *illustration* 126

Another Field - *illustration* 128

No Strings 130

My Tree - *illustration* 132

Sheila and Ralph - *illustration* 136

Ripe Fruit - *illustration* 140

Locked Long 143

Looking Out - *illustration* 144

On Unseen Wings - *illustration* 146

You Reminded Me 148

Sharp Shards - *illustration* 150

Changed My Ideas - *illustration* 152

Those Days 153

Some Shadow - *illustration* 154

The Day You Returned 156

Things Unspoken 157

Robin Herald - *illustration* 158

Personally - *illustration* 159

A Little Place - *illustration* 162

Mind's Eye Palette - *illustration* 164

Memories - *illustration* 166

Love Sentence - *illustration* 168

Why - *illustration* 171

The Planets 174

The Only Way 175

Passed That House - *illustration* 176

Unforeseen Rocks - *illustration* 178

Strange Tricks - *illustration* 180

Know I Will - *illustration* 182

Lost Glory - *illustration* 184

Often - *illustration* 186

Garden Delights, (for Kate) - *illustration* 188

Words For a Bereaved Friend - *illustration* 192

Heart's Seasons 194

Wish For A Friend - *illustration* 196

First line Index 199

About the Poet and Artist 205

We Stood With the Stars

Think we lay in that meadow

Amongst the flowers, high

Earthly together

Some centuries gone by

And when we stood with the stars

Our essence was as one

You, another twinkling

Maybe an age yet begun

And I hear your soft notes

I reach out with my hand

You were the constant mirage

Through the shifting sand

And in that bright fire

I felt your breath warm with mine

Elemental always then

And until a future time

The Wild Horse

When was the wild horse broken

Fire taken from his eyes

High places forbidden

Wide vistas hidden

Lost days of surprise

Predictable pathways

Masters in control

How to now reclaim

Get back and regain

A buried broken soul?

Show me the wild mountain

Bright meadows below

Perfumes, forest spirit

Feelings hidden in it

That I forgot to know

Deep inside the heart

Lost somewhere long ago

Is still old desire

Fighting burning fire

A wild thing needs to know

Shadow Times

In some old world, lives ago

Smiles adorned happy faces,

Minutes between leave traces,

Unseen in what we may show,

Shadow times, lost embraces

East winds cut, blow cruel chill,

Familiar other you found,

Mystic world of special sound,

Does love warm your sad soul still?

Did early joy stay around?

Fire can keep lit, burning hot

Some ideas surprise, survive

Flickering, dim, fanned alive,

Pictures flames never forgot,

Dreams born only to deprive

When the path was hard to find
A way harsh, cold, so unclear,
How far away was how near?
Memory etched in the mind
A past not forgotten year

In the new world here today
Life's lines sadness just can't hide,
And ghosts in pale mists divide,
Words emerge so late to say
Were kind thoughts kept deep inside?

Did you know you held the key?
Hear secrets long buried, mine,
Lines in a love song entwined,
Some strange realm, word irony
With my fate and you I find

Trod These Paths

Fish forever swimming east

Underneath my bath

Same as the cold grey tortoise

On my green garden path

David stands in the shadow

Beneath the birch, Ron's tree

Trod these paths forever

Mysterious gnomes smile at me

Spirits, although here are resting

Fur and memories gone to earth

Send their life to my days now

Kaleidoscope confirm their rebirth

The Keys

The keys came across time down to me -

Old gates, wooden doors, private spaces,

Handmade, several tiny, others huge

Once held by fingers in unknown places

Some wrought fine or cast in iron, strong

Made in brass - keys with ancient power,

The access to silent seclusions

Or secret lock to a gilded tower

Safe in old pockets, or on a hook

Imbued with joy, emotion or fears

Their depths speak new echoes to me now

Yet unused for over a hundred years

Didn't dream, or know, I'd realise -

Long line hanging high along my hall,

That I'd discover one was missing

And the most important key of them all

Forest Hollows

Was it a sound as well as a feeling
Down at the still river's edge
Left behind in the rush of years,
Inside the gnarled grey tree, leaning
Across dark water welled with tears

Always heard a hushed teasing silence,
Magical notes distant calling
Knowledge deep buried with hope flawed
Unearthed, futile hidden pretence,
Faith's forgotten low minor chord

In forest hollow secret lonely spaces
Music muted, too far away,
Sounds – time's elements could remake
Find abandoned tattered traces
Reaching heart asleep, yet awake

A warm breeze blew softly back upon me
Released damaged demons to light,
Rekindled thoughts lost and adrift
Psyche spark - blue soul with that key
Called quiet, brought creation's gift

Hard hailstones are now melting here,
Joy and pain so close together,
Fell fast in the water today,
Spirit of love which cancels fear
Inspires thanks more than I can say

Hidden Lives

How deep are our hidden lives

Dreams dusty but still alive

Discovered waiting in ambush

Wild oceans in my eyes

The promise of the sun and moon

Hopes hidden, desires dashed

Quicksilver on soft breezes

Bonfire that burnt too soon

Shadow looking for the door

Smile evaporating mist

Masquerading freedom

Leaving much less, not more

Words, too few years ago

Shadow man you remain

So how is it, a mystery

You make me so high, so low

Not here but you touch me

What was it really then

Dreams dusty still alive

Twin souls of eternity?

All the Times

Saw that black, deep dismal puddle

Thought is this made of suppressed tears,

All the times I refused to cry

Smoked away secret and hidden fears

The person smiling over years

Always encouragement and words,

No advisor for the advisor

Unspoken thoughts never heard.

The sparrowhawk came down today

Blood of the young white feathered dove

And suddenly surprise, I find

Others do care, and send their love.

Tiny trees planted, now proud and tall,

Shoots show green, Spring will be soon,

Colours hide, paints waiting all this time,

I'll look bright up to the crescent moon

Two Lives

Here I am hostage with this naked soul
Never washed clean on rough tides
Know the same feeling is flooding in,
An old voice in my heart still abides

Thought of that house there, near to the sea
North, summer, when something went cold,
Unlined our faces – but still the same me,
You know I'm love's idiot 'til I am old

Have I the courage to say this to you -
Candid heart meets your mystery,
Strong and wise, but you already know
With your secrets well-hidden from me

Silence slices my thin resolve
Fights hard against any good sense,
Pointless now as it ever was then
You wiped out all my lines of defence

Dreams demolished those years ago

Are cancelled out by you here today

There's no blame ever, just two lives

And things that get caught on the way

The Magic

Is yesterday's illusion

Haunting me still?

That misty confusion

Following the thrill

Like a passing cloud

Felt the lonely chill

Mist obscured in my mind,

Was I silent, too proud

Or always one breath behind?

So lost summer days

My dreams, but not yours,

A spectre in the rays

Peering back through frayed gauze

How did you touch me?

Somewhere deep in my soul,

So today's reality

Was never quite a whole,

Wondering winter time

That chill hidden there

An essence not a crime

Words - maybe you do care,

I find old desires

Touch me, as if they're new

Ashes turned into fires -

Must be the magic of you

The Crow, Hippocampus and the Angel

Murmuring birds high in the mighty oak

Fresh with mimosa fragrant warm breeze,

Was it a lofty smart crow I can thank

Who dropped that gift down there from the trees

Upside down on the gently sloping bank?

Just a squarish piece, pottery, dull white

I felt compelled to investigate:

A hippocampus, dragon of the sea

A rough fragment – part off an old plate

Brought especially by a bird just for me

A divine strand, a precious link beyond
Old glazed black, white and gold broken shard,
In the brain it's the part helps us create,
Here heraldic, on a shield with bars
Once part of a very fine ancient plate

And as I wandered my eye saw the twinkle
Shining, tiny glint caught by sun's rays
Yes, I do think the birds left it just there
I was seeking strength - a new way -
A silver angel hands together in prayer

Songs divine, the birds emanate spirit
From the trees they are watching always,
When we need help or a sign they reach out
Connect magic strands kissing new days,
Invisible souls link us here - no doubt

Threads Still Run

I saw a distant shadow

A ghost in the grey gloom

Yet something was familiar

When I saw that sad old room

Wide and deep the hollow

In the cold and lonely ground

I buried years of lost dreams

I had lost what I had found

Glittering the cold water

Salt sad tears of rolling foam

Pale lonely sun of pity

Left me cold and so alone

I knew you weren't perfect

Never straight, kind or true

But you held the magnet

That drew me back to you

I saw the cage that held you

Your young evasive heart

Yet threads still run between us

And arrows they still dart

Now the geese fly over

The wide v in the sky

So love can last forever

Although buried didn't die

Venus and Mars

Glimmering gold sun rays

Lights clouds like veils of lace,

Seabirds low, soar crying

Feathered freedom, flying

Towards horizon haze,

Distant time, unknown place

Droplets, gentle shower

Rainbow prisms, arcs of light

Softly glance, kiss grass, green,

Forgotten world, unseen,

Ancient leisured long hour

Fragranced with wild delight

Orange flickering fire

Dance high, reach bright the stars

Rising brilliant hot flames

Mystery, love's games,

Crackling laughing choir

Dazzle Venus and Mars

Fleeting shadows tracing

Alchemy of the heart,

Adonis, Aphrodite

Magic timeless psyche

Eternal, embracing

Petals red, torn apart

Reflection

My spirit I surrendered

In battle – a myth, not won

End with no beginning

A life never begun

Dreams no longer spinning

Ripe harvests left unsown

A world of love not planted

Flower seeds that never shone

Dusty illusions

Felt by only one

With buried delusions

So long past and gone

A strange sensation

Blew through my soul again

Watch the birds fly high

A world of joy and pain

The truth hides with the lie

But before the sun is rain

Facets

Is it like a diamond

Or the black heart of coal,

Facets of our selves

Parts that make us whole

Are we any of these,

Are any of them more?

Breezes blowing by

Washing waves on the shore

When I send you love

Does it reach so far?

Across the wild woods

Spirits sleeping in the stars

Gaze at the night sky

Tell me so tonight

I'll hear you laughing

And it will be alright

Let the Dryads Play

Just keep away from the cliff's edge
Now they are crumbling away
Peep fast in that thick, dark forest
Don't go in, let the dryads play
And when you walk by the tunnels
Where ancient miners lie and moan
Watch where you put your footstep
Hidden shafts go many miles down
And if you are out on moorland
Careful, keep to the footpath track
Wander out over the wild green hills
You might find it too hard to get back
But then looking out from your burrow
Over the edge of the steep unknown
You might glimpse the forgotten pathway
Where dreams on the mists have blown

A Hidden Husk

You found the forgotten silent seed

In dull overgrown wasted acres

A hidden husk of abandoned hope

Joy long lost, lonely and forsaken,

Fate or spirits calling once again

Hear music distant but ever there

Magic returned, golden strands so near,

Times gone between dissolved in new air

Fiery Fate

You said you had a bet with the devil,

Or was it a dance tempting fiery fate?

And you thought you had triumphed, won the deal:

But now – is the horizon still level?

Was there harsh laughter at the furnace gate?

Had sly Nick stirred dark plans: more treasures to steal?

Sweet - you play smooth, eternal emotions,

Softly pluck then sing of them in your songs,

Weave timeless beauty through chords and verses,

But was brimstone being mixed with dark potions,

Yellow flames crackling prodded by sharp prongs,

Sealed blazing with covert future curses

You love life, the beautiful view you see,
Wide vistas new or some past reflection
Shimmering unclear in the deepest well,
Can we create our delights endlessly?
And who lifted that latch of connection?
Thin gap between heart's high heaven or hell

That one hard-won wager, was well-achieved,
But did you then look ahead and behind?
Hear the snap of rough dry smouldering sticks,
A battle glory, so hoped and believed,
But silent, stealthy, underserved, to find
A cruel force lurked plotting more secret tricks

Looking Longer Back

I haven't been a saint,

Knelt down at any shrine

Loved to smoke cigarettes

Take extras with my wine

Looking longer back now

Call me that stupid fool

I broke the rules and laughed

Distanced myself with cool

Made that bed together

I see it now so clear

But love walked far away

The shadow disappeared

I peer inside your soul

Recognise pangs of pain

I'll stay safe in my cave

Can't go back there again

Here's my cerebral self

My muse now calling me

How can fate play such tricks

When no leaves are on the tree?

Still in my Mind

Pristine white canvasses
Paintings still in my mind
And looking to the distance
Is much harder now I find

All the lovely fabrics cut
To make a quilt, my first
A see-saw survival of
Hoping for best not worst

Tumbling words in my head
Yet unwritten on a page
How many will stay within
Impossible to gauge

Jasmine and roses
Will I see them bloom
Or is my last tomorrow
Suddenly too soon

Seasons with great beauty
Sea, the trees and sky
Is it something I must forfeit
And say too soon goodbye

New garden landscape
Seen in my mind's eye
Birds, bees and perfumes
Or a dream passing by

Deep unspent passions
Of both heart and mind
Overwhelm my senses
Hard tears make me blind

Words yet unspoken
Wishes unfulfilled
Seeds of love unsown
Harvest ground untilled

Want to hear new music

Heart-rending, that voice

Feel helpless and unsure

If I even have a choice

I see the bright colours

The scene is set so bold

Yet wisdom's telling me

Some do not grow old

Here I am shivering

Quaking at my fate

Dreams of a new way with

Hope it's not too late

A Silent Street

Somewhere on a silent street
A place with two signs there:
One was hope, and one defeat,
Mist moved in so unaware,
Mystery disguised that place
Only one name then remained
Left the hidden clues to trace
The lost key could be regained

Summer Song

Is 'Altruism' the name of my boat?
No it's 'Love' – with timbers made from words
They speak to help row you back afloat
With thoughts once more to be freely shared

Swans white will glide smoothly alongside,
Summer songs rise high notes on the bank,
When time is right, then you will decide
Know I will again be saying thanks

Reach out when a new moon is ready
Until that time I'll wait patiently
Hear me whispering in the eddy
Thanks twice for rescue, you set me free

That Young Guy

So many days slipped by since we met
I was young, just about fifteen,
You walked with me back home that night
And initially you were so keen,
We both laughed, liked what we'd seen
Then you revealed depth and insight

You asked me some questions and smiled,
Such as: "What do you want to be?"
"Visiting buildings, old places,
Living in a bus, going to see
What I can learn about history,
Art, love in green open spaces"

"Oh", you said, "you are much too wild,
And you really write poetry?
Well I want some kids and a wife -

You also want to make pottery?
Meet a guy then not at all like me -
That's another quite different life"

And my heart is heavy right now
Think of a vanished muse, gone long -
Too swiftly a light, then just shadow
Taking away the art of his song,
Lost in the land where old dreams hang
Gold treasures I couldn't watch grow

The words today they now haunt me
That quote, 'To thine own self be true',
Or was it 'fool yourself if you dare'
The kaleidoscope turned deep blue,
Keep on and forget about you -
But does the road yet lead somewhere?

Young Bird

Palest light blue first fresh summer sky,

Yellow streaks of joy, beauty, life lines,

Young bird, proud bright eye, spread her soft wings

Felt inside she knew everything,

White feathers, sailed to perfect clouds high,

Stars clearly revealed fate's pure gold signs

Sunset soft rose glow swift disappeared

Saw the harsh purple sky eclipsed, stark,

Storm swept in cold shadows to lost space,

Restriction now replaced her sure grace

She could no longer glide high and feared,

Hope shattered, desolation was dark

The others soared high on the soft breeze,

Quiet, watched as they flew away free

Somewhere inside was a missing song,

Alone, she'd never truly belong

Vanished, flown far with her heart's ease,

No new leaves would unfurl on her tree

Feathers faded tired grey and tattered,

The forest stayed thick mud in deep mist

Constant torrent of fast rushing rains,

Escape flight futile trapped in thorn chains

Drowned the pathway clear that most mattered,

Branches tangle, contort, hold and twist

Speckled shadows and long reflections

Amongst acorns and dusty brown leaves,

Sun shines fire orange at some distance

Light on each wild dawn of existence,

Music lifts high a heart's connections,

Love remains as life's mystery weaves

Another Moon

Why not another moon – younger with love and light

No brambles across the path, but small perfumed pinks

A way found easier – kind words that forge new links

Not the wolf moon glaring, wild howling in the night

Maybe you only passed my way, curiosity - young lust,

Was I too silent, mesmerised by all that I couldn't say?

Stolen moments from a heart held tight in captivity,

Me then and now, perhaps asking, loving you too much

Our Days

The scars and the sorrow

Wild sea rush inside

Helpless dark hollow

No place now to hide

Black lost tomorrow

Ocean cold much too wide

Tears blue and sharp pain

Penetrate lonely days

Rational, insane

Balanced blind and crazed

Huge tiny bright grain

Unseen not erased

Our days, just how long,

With trials ahead

Can we remain strong

Or buckle instead

Feel we do belong

Or new seasons dread?

Steep downward dark hill

Regret rolls with despair,

Climb back up until

The view is good there

Magic won't stay still

Life is short, so beware

The Phoenix

I must see the phoenix

I painted long ago

With new days ahead

Not yesterday's shadow

Kept that smile and showed

The word my composure

Now I share my secrets

Heartfelt disclosure

How could I ever know

I forgot how to dream

What I lost could return

Find all was not as it seemed

But have I paid the price

For my long masquerade

Consequences, nightmares

A lifetime charade

Couldn't do it another way

Got to this day somehow

Felt you return once again

That dream so real now

Don't tell me I'm Icarus

Only want to feel the sun

Tell me I'm the Phoenix

And that life has just begun

Watch the Tides

Surely the sinners can't be that thing

That follows never-ending youth?

Want all that life will yet bring,

Look away now deny a truth

When your mind is overflowing

With love and tomorrow's plans

Do we know without knowing?

Watch the tides and drifting sands

And still, in the dusk of morning

Distant, saw a soul out there

See purple skies will be soon dawning

Some other fresh day with less care

Dark spirit low, aware, in pain,

Loves lost swept in wild whirling wind,

Vivid colours return, regain

And the sinners haven't yet sinned

A Wish For You

Linger just lightly, listen as the sun rises

When a small bright bird sings sweet, I hope you will smile:

May nature restore your full strength in a short while

To fight battles ahead as hard fate devises

Softly perfumed waves float heady in spring rain

Colours vivid life sparkle new ideas effect,

Raindrops refresh your weary soul joy to connect

Find direction to replace deep sorrow and pain

When the slower breath of evening's dim daylight drifts

See the stars shine again as the sky darkens hue,

May heaven's inspiration then safely guide you

With a generous share of green, glorious gifts

And lost in the silent darkest moments of sleep

May golden dreams hold you with gentle memories

To carry pure peace and a calm heart at ease,

Treasures tied up with love to long cherish and keep

The Wild Place

Why am I climbing the steep hill
Searching the view and the sea
Looking to find that special place
Then discovering it's not for me

Why am I running to the forest
Dizzy perfumes of trees delight
Disappearing on the southern breeze
With old spirits just out of sight

What takes me back to the wild place
Dark grey roaring and angry shore
Suddenly I knew the answer
I'd seen it there once before

I dashed into green meadows
Knew that right here I do belong
And through the trees just gently
Heard the magic of your song

Doubt You Ever Knew

Doubt that you ever knew

How hard your loss hit back then,

Bent low, away my dreams blew,

The tide never left the shore,

Somehow I loved you more

Years whirled on, fast and slow,

Cold currents, vast fathoms dark

Washed rolling waves, etched echo,

Always the one word it said,

Same name in heart and head

Mermaids called, did you hear

Far songs drifting on oceans,

Night distant, yet always near,

Searching flowing evermore

Faint whispers on golden shores

Aware forever - missed,

Chasing grey clouds still today,

Lips warm sun had hardly kissed,

Heart's voice, fire mind, spark - your eyes,

Listen - hear mermaid's cries

Doubt back then you could know,

Ached dreams so long resonate,

Silent secrets sleeping grow,

Soul shreds not swept to sea,

Lives unlived, for eternity

Will You Take A Walk

Will you take a walk with me,
Feel the soft raindrops fall?
Can I watch you playing,
Will I hear you call?
Can we feel the sun's glow,
Gently warming heat?
Watch clouds together,
Where will we meet?
Gaze at those stars bright
Laugh in the magic air?
When I glance around
Will you be standing there?
Look, see the horizon
Where the seagulls fly
Like my imagination,
Reaching for the sky

My Lost Way

Too kind and strong, for all the rest

Now what strength is left for me?

I see the stars, I see the test

Here now, and it's haunting me,

Strength, yes, so much to spare,

But where has it gone today?

I was the one, always there

But lost myself along the way,

Have I still enough in reserve

To climb back up the hill,

Or was I one just born to serve

Always to subjugate my will,

When did I forget who I was

Ignore inner need, desire?

How to regain the vanished loss

Reignite the dampened fire?

Hope I can find my lost way back

And live life as I wanted to

An abandoned lost narrow track

Not quite yet come into view

November Dreams

Venus low, bright in the western sky

And your voice, hearing now, real with me,

November dreams or telepathy -

Do minds exceed physicality?

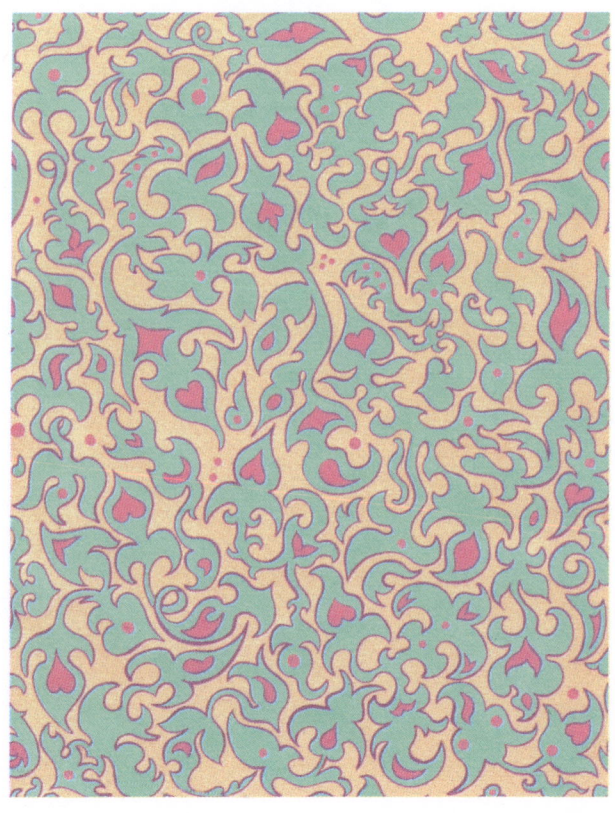

Spider Spins a Web

The years seen to others often belie

That true contentment and calm peace prevails,

Rainbow reflects, flowered haven thinks most,

Imagined ideal mocks unequal tie,

Balance was lost back in wild howling gales,

Stone wall was here with the gardener's ghost

A pattern lived before, people long flown,

Earlier tales told of rifts and heartache,

Heard back then, sounded removed, rather strange,

But things have vanished since, remained unknown,

Yesterday's hope is the present's mistake

Along with certainty we don't all change

No magic it seems can stop time's harsh gale,
Dust is the last resting place of high dreams,
One has the losses, so one has the gains,
The circle turns, reveals the same tired tale
Where joy and love become lost in between,
A dominant force holds tight to the reins

Spider spins a web, intricate fine thread
Dewdrops jewels a sure trap lies in wait,
Silent space of tunnels shrunken in size,
No pathway points where lost footsteps have led,
Locate the door before it gets too late
Though the dusk has stolen light from my eyes

At the Crossroads

Now at the crossroads
I'm seeing with new eyes
Game of charades and
Mask dropped, tired disguise

Standing today again
And this time first,
Looking towards the better
And leaving behind the worst

Almost broken spirit,
Did it have to be this way?
Hope for new path
Where I'm no longer coloured grey

Now at the crossroads,
Route I can't clearly see
But when it appears
It will be the one for me

Took such a long time

To find my way here

Here at the crossroads

Hope soon it will be clear

Priestess

Said I was a priestess
Or leader of some cult,
Wonder was I cruel
Then and retribution
My present life's result

Tears cried always alone
Emotion's lonely ditch,
Rainbow never sparkled
Set to weep divided,
Karma's a callous bitch

Said I was born psychic
Future so well mapped out,
But magic escaped me,
A spell I'd have conjured,
With high dreams, have no doubt

Smile, sing, laugh every day

Hide it cool like new snow,

Feel the well there inside

Just don't ever reveal,

Same for me too… I know

The Other Ones

Dazzle, shimmer peacocks

With your jewels over-bright

Strut and preen those feathers

Reflect your surface light

Wear your careful jewels

What you need to show

Smile glimmering vision

Admire the one you know

Look in the muddy water

Delight in your reflection

Gaze for happy hours

Nothing short of perfection

Then avoid the meadow

Where the wild flowers grow

It's a foreign land

Where the other ones go

And in the darkness

Just keep well away

Danger hides in blackness

Just dazzle every day

Around the corner

Lying in the shade

Are the ragged ones

True and unafraid

Let them look inside

Places you'll never know

Things you will reap come

From the seeds you sow

That Dublin Evening

Cycling long miles to Dublin
Hunger was greater than summer heat
Found somewhere late in the city, quiet,
Locked the bikes and then found a seat

Grey beard – eyes lighting his corner
He sat down near: "My name's Maitland Woolf",
Spoke in bright ribbons of conversation
Spanning the ages and cultural gulf

Said: "Why are you two together:
I can see that your stars aren't aligned",
We laughed and said we'd asked ourselves
That same question, oh, many times

"I own an antiquarian bookshop
I lecture at the Uni. and see
You are the one I've been searching for -
It's for you, follow your true destiny"

I knew of magic, he quoted a verse
Imprinted long still on my mind;
Said "I knew Aleister Crowley way back;
You're special - took me so long to find"

Was I the young coward who wouldn't leap
Out of familiar unsettled days?
Often I think back to that Dublin evening
Felt him sad as I watched, walk away

And slow, his old figure receding
With grey hair and his walking cane
I knew he was my childhood drawing
And our stars would never cross again

Seagulls Scream

Seagulls scream now every morning

Takes me by surprise

Were they always crying before?

Or specially flown from the shore

To a thing they recognise?

Children laughing, carefree playing

Echo memories past,

Squeals knowing warm love

Drifting to me lost, above -

Reluctant truth, nothing lasts

Wild whistling windy evening

Groans, swirling moaning gusts,

Urgent, unforgiving

Excitement of living,

Passions passing and spent lusts

Bending trees whispering breezes
Stories, crackling rhymes,
Brittle branches snap
As memories overlap
Of tales told at other times

Crazed cool silver mirror shining
Reflecting dim in a haze,
Shadow ghosts appear
Humming hidden fear,
Hints of dreams never erased

Night time asleep, the song came
Softly, magic muse this way,
Safely held me safe there
Close and calm, aware -
New notes of another day

The Truth

In some space just hiding there

Is love that never died

Captured me then unaware

Yet so long since denied

Uneven is a heavy load so

Just best to try and hide

Tears will never balance

However many cried

Lost in that endless ocean

With never ebbing tide

Dreams floating on the water

That never will subside

The mind did play tricks but

Unhappily it lied

The truth was never hidden

Despite the fact I tried

Lurking there and waiting

It's still alive inside

Passions meeting halfway

The path with the divide

Pluck the courage somehow

Swallow buried pride

But the arrow always misses

The aim is still too wide

Whispered unreality

Sad echo amplified

A heart and mind untouched

Never will be satisfied

Because remaining ever there

Is a love that never died

The Fourth One

Met a minstrel boy with a smile
But an old sorrowful heart,
Went deep in the ancient forest:
Lonely day just disappeared,
Charmed the air, fire and water,
His bed became the earth,
Invoked love and mysteries,
Music's magical kind seer

Think once you said love was like
An old and favourite jumper;
Three flames flared up again this year
From my lost forgotten space,
Hello – goodbye – long lost lovers –
I'd heard one of you was dead.
But from tall trees the fourth one was
The minstrel with the timeless face

I'd been looking in the forest,

Staring miles out to sea,

Knew something had been darkening

Deep, so lost inside my soul,

Flowers, their petals were falling

Into sad Autumn, lines of life,

Never knew the music minstrel's

Missed missing words could make me whole

The Scale

The scale, single feather sits by blackest boulder

The distance too far, suddenly in sharp focus

Youth's quick energy or something lost and colder

Reality or vivid dreams, pleasure enfolds us

Bird bright high song or wild scream too loud for thinking

Smiling complete joy or lined and wretched frowning

Petal floats light and fresh, or ancient ship sinking

Laughing rippling waters or crying oceans drowning

Barbed wire grey wasteland or green field of wild flowers

Damp cave dark with bats release soaring butterflies

Eternity forever or allotted hours

World full of new promises or pit for the unwise

Wandering lost somewhere then strangely understood

A heart left on shore rescued by a kindred soul

A hand, in time reaching strong out across the flood

Discovering, admitting what can make the whole

A stranger far away, yet familiar somehow

Strings low-playing, psyche muted secrets, emerge, real

Thousand old moons dimmed, waned to new crescents now

Touch untouched but magic, a close imagined feel

Fog hiding visions, crystal, no longer remote

Fragrance forgotten, catch the breeze, a lost delight

Concealed sound reveals such beautiful unheard notes

Of perfect peaceful days, blissful harmony nights

Silent Fight

Cold and frightened, I've ambushed myself

Narrow tunnel, trying hard to escape

But when did I turn into someone else

Alone in this barren landscape

Catching water drips in the night

Calling out for a far other voice,

Only myself in this silent fight

Will the outcome be of my choice?

Many colours crowd in my mind

Fear they might now turn to grey

Must look forward and not behind

Face the future that begins today

Crows Early Call

Crows early call from the roof ridge
Greeting caws, they speak to me,
Know I tried hard to save the life
Of their giant ancestral tree

Black, alert eyes see me waving
Reply daily and call 'hello',
Parade today on the high point
They talk of something we both know

Shared horizon changed in one day,
Cutters removed their towering perch,
But not my friends the shining crows,
Loudly return, tell me to search

Coal handsome feathers, dark radiance,
Span long years, old intelligence,
Remember those dreams held before
Twilight reveals without pretence

Dormant

Dormant, still and buried, underneath dead leaves and years

Of searching for something missing, unknown, with no name

A dusty page never lay flat in the hidden book

Obscured, unreachable, denied colour, trace or claim

Maybe I looked through labels, there wasn't one that fit

Searched and saw the long lists, so many clues, not a word

No hint of that once silver strand, long tied, tangled, lost

Memories of music, so far distant never heard,

Survival by amnesia, honest cold part of it

Box of tears, dreams and sadness, nailed up so long ago

Rusting in cold ground, ignored, many crescent moons rose

Until the sun gave buried seed a new day to grow

Wish With Me

A day fresh and beautiful
I'll see your eyes in the light
Smell the green world of joy
A wrong world turned right
Look through that window
See the glorious sky
With light shining for us
Watching clouds up high
We'll smell the flowers
Even if it's pouring rain
Enjoy some time together
Treasured you and me once again
Don't know the date though
Can only hope it's not too far
Look later at the night sky
Wish with me – see that star

Remember

Alone in that big hall

Fanlight frightening up there

Just about three or four

Sitting alone on the stair

Remember how it felt

Looking objectively

Wondered why it was

So deep inside of me

Asked myself this question

Young, but I couldn't say

Just how did it happen

That I cried every day?

And why was I happy

All alone in the wood

Then forgot about joy

A life misunderstood

Bow down with the breeze

Stormy days are ahead

Run from the storm

Don't choose life dead

Should have listened then

Known there was a choice

Melancholy dreamer

Deaf to her inner voice

Catch the Water

Catch the water yesterday

The deluge and the dart

See now if your hands get wet

Hear tears cry in your heart

Running rivers call us in

Into the ocean wide

Horizon spinning on the sea

Bring the blue deep inside

Catch the high wind in the trees

Dashing amongst brown leaves

Pages of memory's laughter

Sorrows, regrets and fears

See that old mirror shining

Catch the image in mind

Remember as you hold it

The sun can make you blind

Perfect cobweb's silver dew

Sparkles light on the thread

Words always left unspoken

Some strange fate decrees instead

Fasten Those Bars Tight

Fasten those bars tight round the bird

Lock the door to the gallery

Deafen the notes of old delights

Hide all the keys away from me

Keep those wings clipped carelessly

Shut fast all the signs of spring

Then tomorrow watch the dawn break

As your bird forgets how to sing

So faint, small smile, ignore the scream

Howl inside, take goodwill and kind

Only look at the path you choose to walk

Wear those blinkers that make you blind

Footsteps trodden by one for two

You are solo down selfish street

Don't ever tell me what I should say

I have plenty of words for defeat

Blind the rocks you put in the road
Useless your old barricades
The goodwill and innate kindness
Grow dim now as old love fades

Choose not to hear my many words
Repeated so endlessly
Just do what you wanted to do
As you so long lost sight of me

The phoenix rose in the morning
Flew high through thick veils of gloom
Unlocked a prison of words and thoughts
Lost laments of long winters doom

Birds can see all in the darkness
Hear kindred spirit call once again
Say fly now as you once meant to,
So thank you my dearest bright friend

Perfume of Roses

Perhaps when there's perfume of roses -
One, yellow, tinged with pink is called 'Peace',
May we feel that spirit and essence,
Give these long months of pain due release

Don't let us mention any sharp thorns,
Just rediscover joy to reclaim,
A friendship, art and maybe some fun
With no need of a tie or a name

In my mind I will see us both there -
Feel the breeze whisper and summer sun,
Pick up some pieces and not let go
Something special, we've hardly begun

World of Words

World of words left trapped inside ancient heart

Leapt over long years, rushed back then beyond

Cold released chains collapse, turn scarlet fire

Icicles melt, hard blue crystals dissolve

Listen now hear that beautiful music,

Mystical notes dance across a new bridge

Toward the mud rutted island tracks deep,

Crescent halo glows new sky a star map

Highlights hope today, dream shapes evolving

Calling To Somewhere

The horse lifted his head on the hillside
Saw thorns and stones on a path unknown,
Wild water, wet rocks, rushing wide,
Calling to somewhere he once denied,
Beckoning, roared: knew his way was alone

Trees thick tangled with boulders beneath
Distant pathway snaked out of clear view,
Felt the tremble of known earth underneath,
Fire caught his mind - blazed sudden relief
Spirit whispered softly what he must do

Gently discover the route far ahead
Fight the narrow thicket way concealed,
Travel, now explore where faith has led
Find another light dream, life instead,
Smiling heart said escape will be revealed

The horse had known one lonely bleak place,

Sodden ground, with mossed greying green earth,

Burnished land beckoned him to chase

To horizons unclear - white mists to embrace

Spring ushered spirit awaiting rebirth

Fool

Fool's looking closer back from the mirror,
Fast flows the ancient river deep, runs full,
Dark waters held hard by rising bubbles,
Numbing, disguised concealed current struggles,
Mossy bank bursts wide, breaking life's long lull

Glass sparkled brightly, another beckoned,
Caressing rose high in its course again,
Pretended that physical endurance
Was an escape, some inbuilt insurance
Against admitting emotional pain

Blanket of bubbles popped years then vanished,
Ran away, fades spirit tide of lost youth,
Recognise the stranger there with new eyes,
Admit a fool revealed, told herself lies,
Reflection pours inescapable truth

I Know

Yes, I know I chose this one,

A life of subjugation

Loneliness became too much

An end to isolation

And why: those first words of yours -

No way to start, but finish

Did I choose this harder life

And my true self diminish?

How did I think this an escape?

The truth, one day I'd find:

The veil was thin, just words away

Not lost in my heart and mind,

Those fickle years of favours

Friends don't know, and call me wise,

Yet in my heart looking now

I see vistas with new eyes,

Yes, maybe I chose the pain

No way to communicate

Must reach in and back and find

Me before it gets too late

Future Days

Several senior ladies smiled in those days
Couldn't believe the luck of some mothers,
"All that you ask, want or fancy, she does,
Even advice - always willing and wise,
Capable and quick, not like others",
But they showed a hint of green in old eyes

Various men would see very clearly
A difference, not at all like their wives:
Gardener, tailor, cook, maid and mentor,
And more, all achieved with a placid smile,
Their words spoke clearly of restricted lives;
The mask hid well that could charm and beguile

Many came along in pain and distress
Whether with an aching body or mind,
Helped feel well, balanced, firm feet back in step,
"Feel reborn, strong again, just like brand new,
In your sanctuary, you are so kind,
Now I see a fresh future, clear way through"

But when the day for me finally arrived,

The gulf of time in between seemed too great,

Heart and mind given so long to others,

Diamonds for me that I just couldn't hold,

Can the soul erode, have too long to wait?

Silence inside felt hard, lonely and cold

But a new dawn lies ahead, future days,

Three things I'm aiming and wishing for still,

Surely easier now, hope they're granted:

To create with fresh colour, a free mind,

Time ahead staying safe, bright and not ill,

And to talk life with a good friend who's kind

One Way Street

Saw that ancient apparition

Tired, sad, hunched on the sandstone wall

Heard the gardener, last century

Gave up, weary, worn with it all

Still crawling slowly just one way

On this old haunted one way street

Watching the empty years flash since

The falling footsteps of those feet

Hearing echoes of dim past times

Resentment still hides dark but clear

Rose scarlet tears buried shallow

Ghosts that suddenly reappear

Deception laughs over instinct

Look beyond, look back with fresh eyes

Hearts let events somehow happen

Fate's sly jokes on the young unwise

Words - that magic link can bind us

Perhaps ones found in yesterday

Back in the lost last century

Turn and look at another day

Love Remains

Footsteps crying as you walk

Heart afraid of the hard road

Haunted by what you have known

No familiar hand to hold

Don't think you are alone now

As you search the way ahead

Souls are with you, loving you

Both the living and the dead

When you take the narrow path

See there's always love inside

Shadow dance in tunes of life

See the pathway open wide

Don't be afraid of shadows

Mirrors will light up the way

Recall yesterday's laughing

And it will help guide new days

You may feel you're deserted

Think joy has forever gone

Love remains always with you

And heard in tomorrow's song

Just Some Yesterday

Morning, the mirage, enveloping haze

It was only a breath before

Just some yesterday,

Route mysterious

Day unclear to us

Colours rising from grey

Through my eye's opening door

Strange enchantment of your ways

Afternoon knew crimson brief fire bright

Just a quick breath on my skin,

Feeling I viewed

Such a short time

My dream sublime

Heart solitude

Left locked, regret within,

Mistaken some wrong for so right

Evening and golden magic was greater

Just a soft new breath apart,

Warmer now today

Still with mystery

As it remains to me,

Yet right words to say

Speak into my heart

Echo an answer of another later

Disease

Disease will strip down any wild delusion
Along with pain in the mind and flesh,
Sadness shows the stark conclusion,
The guise of love will always enmesh

Have heard talk of rare selfless guys
Happy to have partners first in mind,
Why me the fool, the one so wise
Who always found the other kind?

Tried in many ways to create pleasure
Sure, and know I did it with a smile,
How then only one had the leisure
Gained off the one who could beguile?

So they call it love, for some perhaps,
Lucky ones who together have grown,
Get ill you might find the smile will lapse
Then you'll wished that you lived alone

Hope springs eternal, we all have dreams,
Always look for the treasure that's right,
Illness tears the harsh truth at the seams
At the point where you least need the fight

So when you recall your high dreamt vision
The happy ever after life hoped for once,
Scorn that folly of yours with derision
Your words gain no sorry or even response

Some men still don't know when to realise
Until your strength is taken elsewhere,
Too late then, reflect where buried love lies,
When you don't return what was everywhere

The Luck

Why did I never find the luck

Some other girls have found,

A guy who'd think of her,

Just now and then...

Instead it's always been

The other way around

Why didn't I have the luck,

Man who knew what made me tick,

To talk long together

Any topic at all...

Not just about his ills,

If ever I was sick

Why didn't I have the luck

To know someone fun and wise,

Help me over hurdles,

Strength of mind,

See how it is for me,

Not his world through his eyes

Why didn't I have the luck

To be with a man who's clever,

Teach me what I missed,

In unspoken ease...

Didn't know unselfish,

And had a meal cooked, never

Why didn't I have the luck

Man with interests, not just his own,

Do some jobs in the house,

Know what's needed...

Instead of leaving me to figure

The best way ahead alone,

Why did I never find the luck

That lovely man of my dreams,

Understanding, calm,

Creative, kind,

Caring arms of warmth...

Other girls had the luck, it seems

In the Desert

You can drown in a desert,
Some might say, 'it's much too dry',
No water and no ocean,
Depends how much you cry

You can feel ice in the desert,
Some might say 'I'm sure you can't',
Depends how many needles
Pierce cold into your heart

You can see trees in the desert,
Some might say 'there's just no way',
Depends on seeds in your mind
You planted yesterday

Flowers grow wild in the desert,
Some might say 'are you quite sure?'
The more you seek out beauty
You see it all the more

Talk with friends in the desert,
Some might say 'surely no chance',
Spirits can speak together
And for that echo thanks

You can starve in the desert,
Some will say 'you won't survive',
Without love and laughter it's
Harder to be alive

See pale ghosts in the desert,
Some will say 'ridges in relief',
No, I'm remembering
Some strands of self-belief

Hear bird song in the desert,
Some will say 'the breezes blow',
No, it's me thinking of
New dreams I need to sow

See the stars shine in the desert,
Glowing sun now rising red,
Lighting a strange pathway -
The future lies ahead

Glances

Glances through the golden glass

Catch a stranger's sparkling eye

Exchange of raw intentions pass

Hot moments caught and an empty sigh

Words whispered nearly yesterday

Hushed secret stolen embraces

Much of nothing to really say

To a mist of forgotten faces

Wild fun and fast fleeting fashion

Dark nights that fate devises

Hollow lost mistaken passion

And tomorrow the Phoenix rises

Baby Dawn

I would not have ever been born

But for the death of baby Dawn,

Only fifteen months alive, so brief,

Parents left shattered in disbelief,

She'd arrived with a caul on her head,

Special, a lucky future lay out ahead,

Sure sign of a psychic, a chosen life,

But fate's plan only delivered strife,

Poisoned – sweet spoilt perfection,

Grave side sorrow, sad reflection;

Long future to cry tears and grieve,

A Mother still so young and naïve,

Her rising fears were all dismissed,

But Doctors, each of them missed

Mercury signs, in the teething powder,

Although her alarm was voiced louder,

Sold for young babies in a chemist shop

But brought many bright lives to a stop;

And they always wanted a girl and a boy,

My parent's perfect dream of family joy,

And after the birth of my golden brother

They wanted a girl to complete, another,

I was told about this tragedy back then

Of smiling beautiful Dawn Vivienne,

So when I drew my very first breath

Later learnt it was only due to her death,

I would not have ever been born

But for the death of baby Dawn

New Red Sunrise

Fountains falling playfully

Unseen in some foreign land

Gentle watered memory

Trickling through my hands

Place I could never see

Only try to understand

Yesterday's easy words

Locked muted far too long

Poetry drifting unheard

A singer and his song

Dreams that were dared

Danger in being wrong

Wood laid ready, unlit fire

Waiting for a distant spark

Heart hope ages pyre

Dry reality's muted mark

Latent buried hot desire

Returning rush after dark

One quiet new red sunrise

I could see the fountain play

Mind's reach, hear soul cries

Words whispering today

Fire burnt and fresh eyes

Saw tomorrow's yesterday

If You Think

Tame only the safest creatures

Safe asleep in a cushioned cage

If you think you can

Take soft whispers and passing whims

Bow well down as the tempests rage

Climb up to that high place you know

Walk alone up the craggy hill

Know you always do

When birds cry shrill and the trees moan

You belong, and they call to you

As clear bright dawn starts singing

Walk to those remembered places

Ask are you alone

Laugh, hear and be with the earth now

With its timeless immortal traces

Another Field

Who could see a full, sure harvest
With viable seed ripe to sow,
Absurd to really imagine
Such wild oats could ever grow

Another field found, fresh and green
Pretty blossom bright grew there,
Lay down youth's faithless head
Bathe in summer perfumed air

Field untilled, ignored, uneven
Stones undisturbed on hard ground,
But hushed among wild flowers
Paradise was already found

Now look again to that dark field
Twisted tree in the corner far
Leaning into sweeping winds,
See where the blaze left that scar

Broken its rough boughs long ago

Leaves deceived the world it healed,

Gaze into the old hollow

Where the truth can be revealed

Clouds drift by across broad meadows

Birds high on the branches sing,

Relating ancient stories

Of seeds lost in some inner ring

No Strings

You caught my eye

That day, a smile full of fun

Little did you know

Your treats had just begun

Such a handsome stranger

On your working day

Call me when you're passing

I'll blow your cares away

Your one bold move

Twinkle, reminiscent

With no strings just laughs

I saw those pale eyes glint

No I won't undress

The thrill is from the maid

My vicarious pleasure

Your dizzy parade

Know I made you wonder

Lost in carnal delight

Yours purely by virtue

Of your eyes, so bright

You took me dreaming

For you I'm a mystery

Yes I blew your mind

Thanks Mr Fantasy

My Tree

Snap the perfect young branch

Old wolf hiding, creeping

Lurking in the low wood

Perverse cold mind leaping

Intentions never good

Cut down that fresh bright growth

Smiling, and you well knew

That your evil actions

Could spoil a pure young view

Cause future dark reactions

Down deep at the slope end

Of my lush childhood wood

Depraved in the dark trees

You so well understood

Took that which you planned and pleased

Hack the fast growing branch

On my own family tree

Young ones go running wild

Searching ways to be free

Witness swift-vanished, the child

Catch me when I'm cornered

Steal my freedom away

My heart will then show you

Love the rest of your days

Long horizon's span askew

Sever fast new shoots there

Vigorous, much too strong

Abide coming seasons

Watch then how I belong

Screaming loud silent reason

And when you think you've done

Finished hard pruning me

All those axes and knives

Won't kill the sprouting tree

Biding alone - still alive

Cut the branches clean off

Which grow from a ringed heart

See sap rise in springtime

This tree will stand apart

Linden flutter, emerald, lime

Songs timeless in the air

Alive high canopy

Love drifting in the crown,

Rise rhythms in the tree

Revealed anew, filtering down

Life circle swirling there,

Soft harmonies high soared

Cancelled times harsh cut back

Branches strong, spirit restored,

Triumph long after attack

Sheila and Ralph

An old village school, very small

Same too with the size of my class,

Two friends were special I recall,

And both shone so incredibly bright,

Exams they easily could pass,

Popular too, kind and polite,

But their lives weren't destined to last

Sheila bookish, dark hair, quiet heart,

Unlike me, naughty and rather wild,

Destined, both studied, very smart,

Ralph - clever, fun, played football so well,

Cute, big brown eyes, was an only child,

His far fate none could see or foretell

Blighted, that splendid future defiled

Ralph was a part of my little gang

We secretly smoked cigs in the park,

Sheila obeyed when the bell rang,

Lived with brothers at her large grey home,

Ralph and I shared a laugh and a lark,

Sheila often sat reading, alone,

But for both life turned horribly dark

Hard to imagine their future plight,

Saw Ralph later, just now and then,

Sheila only the once, gave an invite,

Dear Ralph became sad as he'd grown,

Shy Sheila first time I'd seen since aged ten,

Spoke sometimes to Ralph on the phone

Then never got a chance again

Life had appeared so very well-mapped,

Success then unravelled, went under,

Sadness overwhelmed, maybe joy sapped,

And unable to tie up life's strands

They then ended, I can just wonder -

Lives surrendered by both their own hands -

Suicides – deep wells of dark thunder

The school is no longer still standing

Or playground of those past childhood games,

Carefree early days, undemanding,

Though plans didn't work out as they should:

I think of those two and their high aims -

Shadows dance where we once played and stood

And fondly I remember their names

Ripe Fruit

Thinking about it just now

Desire or a fancy,

Perhaps a small softer spot,

In pleasure that did persist:

With such fruit ripe on the bough,

Tasted well - savoured a lot -

Too hard often to resist

Came in all shapes, odd sizes,

Many of them well-enjoyed,

Sometimes too much I know,

Clever, handsome, short or tall

Occasionally with guises,

Reflect later what you sow,

Thoughts for autumn's quiet fall

Yes of course perhaps it's true,

Some might remark why bother,

Delight has so many names

Love the close touch, sounds, and smell,

Especially with one or two,

Cause no hurt – attach no blame,

Be mutually kind as well

Never was a short supply

Of laughter, fun with a smile

Most were very good to know

Satisfaction just to see,

But always at the goodbye

As they left those times to go

I knew none of them knew me

Out in the forest woodland

A far figure disappears

Vanishing beyond the trees

Shadow glimpsed between green leaves,

No goodbye, no waving hand

Mystery footsteps he weaves:

He nearly knew me, I believe

Locked Long

If you asked was I ever romantic, no, just not my style,

The answer would be a grim laugh with a quick shake of the head,

Warm hugs welcomed surely, off an old friend not seen for a while?

And kisses? See a swift move, turning the other way instead.

Behind blue icicles, waiting to melt, dissolve or shatter,

Some things are locked long within, in deep hidden secret spaces,

Only one reply could be the one that would really matter,

You can ask, but the world will never see our unseen faces

Looking Out

Face still pressed sad at the glass
Looking out or looking in,
Saw the warm fire burning there
Admit I never could quite pass,
The book lay open, dusty, grey,
Forgot the page with jagged tear -
Upon which words appeared today

That library I still clearly see
Looking in not getting out,
Wisdom speaks of hidden loss,
Long mislaid old rusty key,
Pretended I was free too long
Hidden deep in dark tangled moss -
Colours shine now vivid and strong

Stars bright speak in the night sky

Looking out and looking in,

Dewdrop spheres reflect the sun

Highlight thoughts in my mind's eye,

Shine crescent moon on me below

Point a new clear way now begun,

Old young dreams born ready to grow

On Unseen Wings

Hidden hopes, where did they fly to?

Parted silent on unseen wings,

Covert in a far dark forest,

Haunted glade where nothing sings,

Wild dreams lost in Spring meadows

Where flowers stayed always in bud,

Pollen that was never touched by bees

Had promise to bloom as they should,

Ideas and feelings unspoken

Left with cold grey stones on the shore,

Trodden and lost in hard waves

Forgotten for evermore,

Smiles solitary, secluded

Blown away on an evening breeze

To the edge of the steep mountain side

Swept into ancient gnarled trees,

Tears that fell fast in the deep lake

Where chill waters never subside,

Returned with a remembrance

Desire of life never lived, that died,

Still a strand bright, ever-golden

Sang memory, strange things lost apart,

And silent so long, I returned there,

To a place hidden away in my heart

You Reminded Me

Years ago I loved someone
Although he told me lies,
Yes, you reminded me,
It's something in the eyes.
His were adorable and
He had great talent too,
A lovely singing voice,
Sounded a lot like you,
Yes I loved him, but he
Left tears in my eyes,
Left, but never told me,
Charming, young, but not wise,
Don't think he cared much,
Not enough to say,
You remind me – that's all,
Memory of yesterday,

He brought me delight, but

Sadness followed joy,

You remind me of him, but

He was almost a boy

I was rather stupid then,

Both had too much to drink,

Yes, you do remind me,

But much lovelier, I think,

And I never hated him

Although he went away

And if I was reminded

Could perhaps love him today,

Strange how it happened,

If I listened to that voice

Tears often overtook me,

Same today, heart with no choice

Sharp Shards

See the sharp shards they're dusty, still lying there

Random and raw on some forgotten old floor,

Look back now: focus, find them, scattered, but where,

Feel jagged edges, more acute than before,

See the fresh turquoise cotton with coloured spots

Dancing warm summer, smiling notes, fleeting, brief,

The truth blindly bare, the have and the have not

Bright colours back now, but in sharper relief,

See unspoken spirit, dreamed inspiration

Deeply lost, more darkly cost, heart gone astray,

Memory, wild moments, mad infatuation

Future notes life ahead could never hear play,

See the bright diamond, recall the inclusion

Flawed facets, rough, fated with fickle fault line,

Left faded sparkle, dull sounds of seclusion

Glitters vivid now, finer with magic of time

See, walk the path alone, again, much later

Where no soft answer calls to reciprocate

Yet the need of the years swirls, returns greater

Love's touch reaches out, perhaps it's not too late

Changed My Ideas

When was the map turned upside down

Words were jumbled and printed faint

When did my face change to a frown

The paint box empty, with no paint,

Was thinking I could not return

Changed my ideas just recently

My muse spoke– said there's more to learn

I've taken long years just to see

Those Days

Only on days with a 'y' in
I question how it is and why,
When did these dreams of you begin?
I wonder do the planets lie?
And on days made up of hours
What is it then I strangely feel,
Close far reach of special powers
That hooked me hopeless on the reel,
There's not a tiny part of you
My imagination hasn't caught
Colour it midnight azure blue
Desires this long time longing thought,
And those days when the rivers flow
What most excites me is your mind:
Will you let me explore it though?
Or must time remain undefined?

Some Shadow

Did you ever glance in a mirror
See some shadow dance away?
Wonder were you loved enough,
Is it something you ask today?

And when you heard a distant echo
Strange notes known once before
Drifting away into the distance
Did your mind try to catch it more?

And dark nights when the breeze blew
Did your spirit feel lost and apart?
Did you ever feel sad, so alone,
Some sun absent within your heart?

When you slept, nights quiet, dreaming
Did you feel the touch of a hand?
Wished that it might continue,
Sensed a soul link, a vanished strand

When you again hear me whisper
With words out across every mile
I'll always say your name with love
And hope you will match my smile

The Day You Returned

Lighter hearted yet sad, the day you returned

A joy undreamed, suddenly turned upside down

Few those days, and through you I relearned

At last I could smile, and know less how to frown

Your strength, shaken spirit, kind love, special ways

Restored something vanished and made my heart light

Looking back and forward now through thick haze

Where's the sun? I find the view is sudden night

Short days back then, shorter days now again

Did your mysterious soul sense a need in mine?

Let's see us in sunshine, it always comes after rain

A longer day, with more love and more time

Things Unspoken

In the dark, hidden secret space,
A place I somehow hid so deep
Haunting eyes looked out once again,
Your timeless melancholy face;
Some things we never catch or keep –
Know harvests we'll not sow or reap –

Things unspoken remain unsaid,
The whistle was shrill, but not heard –
Blowing far in forbidden lands,
Voices alive, but they were dead,
Silent songs sung, without a word.
Visions vanished, no longer dared

I saw them yesterday once more –
Daylight lifts the dense veil of night,
Now leaves blow, wildly in the wind,
Just like a thousand years before
Fluttering just beyond my height,
Painted a canvas that's still white

Robin Herald

Dawn was just then emerging

Waning moon vivid, gleaming high

Lacework swaying bare branches

Timeless, beauty – dark blue sky

Robin herald sang clear, unseen

Far passions and passing phases

Perfect moment in a lifetime

Of lost lunar tattered traces

Personally

Personally

Speaking just as me:

How can I be

That state, happy

Although I see

Quite incredibly

You set me free

But then sadly

And currently

Have been cast low

Heartache black blow

Stabbed with sorrow

Told me it's so

Tragic I know

Silence speaks slow

Words must forego

Desires overthrow

But even though

Once acted you dead

Dream dust in my head

Heart that had bled

Your wished-for tread

Knew absence instead

Future to dread

Something I'd said?

What is ahead?

Fate's with the moon

Give light kill gloom

Hope she shines soon

Brings back your tune

Old afternoon

Fun memory

Bright you I see

Missed endlessly

Need setting free

Soul cries a plea

Return happy

Feel harmony

Say it will be

With you I'm strong

No, it's not wrong

Spirits belong

A cloud blue song

Don't be too long

A Little Place

There's a little place in my heart,
Somewhere that's really just quite small,
Pity someone stands well apart
With me that minor part in thrall

There's a minute place in my mind
Only a tiny hiding place,
Although strangely now I do find
Deep there I see that handsome face

There's a passing part during my day
Memory, maybe a short pause, while
I recall some of the words you say
And find that often they make me smile

There's a time, a gold gap in my dreams,
Just fleeting by, although I'm asleep,
A voice sings so sweetly there it seems,
Lovely moments I wish I could keep

There's a remote part inside my brain

Where I'm very honest, usually,

Well, maybe I'm not now and again

And even tell some white lies to me

There's a small secret spot in my soul,

Choose not to go there every day,

Single part that was never a whole

Yet long wished it was another way

Mind's Eye Palette

Carthamus pink, viridian pale hue,

Palette washed clean ready another time,

Recalled to my mind's eye love's secrets untold:

Seaside dreaming, water cobalt pale blue

Brushed in breezes scented with chartreuse lime,

That great dazzling day - orange marigold

Bengal rose summer rush and the pink thrill

Flame red passions alive burnt forever

Under the grove there, spring leaves, linden green

Stays emerald fast imprinted until

Turquoise fades, my tomorrow is never,

Kaleidoscope turns lamp black what I've seen

And felt in magenta wild rose tyrien days,

Naples yellow glows light ochre sun skin

Speckled with parma violet sweet perfume,

Chinese orange dance lit white dappled haze

Magic geranium lake we drowned in,

Crimson vision in my perfect mind room

Memories

You looked at the line drawings
Houses from another time
Do you know the memories
Etched so hard in every line?

Black and white, so unlike life
Dark black in defeated years
Thinking of what might have been
Washed away by bitter tears

Was it just a passing fling
Looking back so very far
Another note idly plucked
On your pensive sad guitar

And if years more lie ahead
Words and music send me light
Pain and joy fight yet again
Hope it will still be alright

And if I never touch your face

I can feel your soul my friend

Maybe again, another life

It might not be meant to end

Love Sentence

Invisible bars encircle my mind

Prisoner of this love sentence,

Rose-tinted or black vision makes me blind

In my masked refusal of repentance

Yet I know my spirit is lonely with this

Love sentence forever to fetter,

Inspiration, collision, old kiss,

Hand-written that unanswered letter

Perhaps pathways fated or chosen

Set barricades around a lost heart,

Vermilion fire flames so swift-frozen

Then a love sentence destined apart

Spin back see memory that excites

Steep avenue before the sharp swerve

Heart that seeks still those hoped-for heights

Is a sentence so pointless to serve

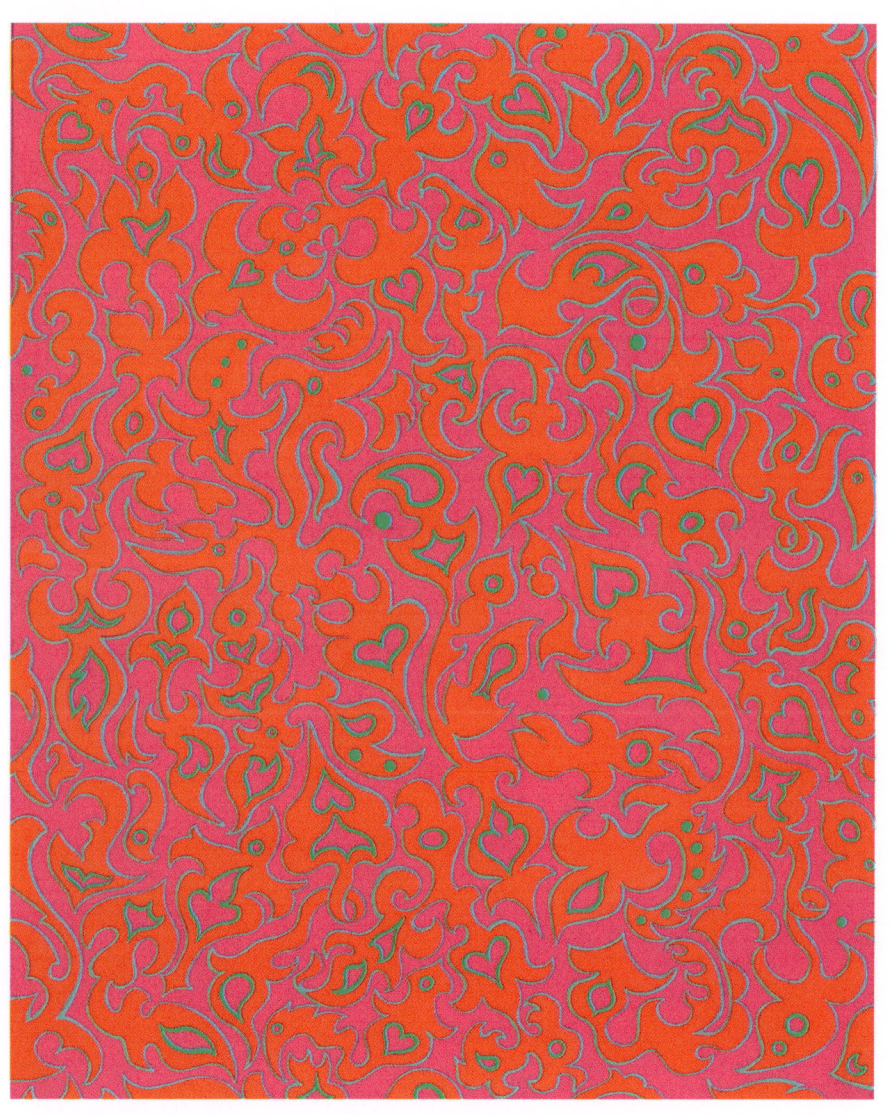

If we could look round lost corners within
Past young heated desires of the flesh
Reason and logic might often win
Not emotions the mind so enmesh

Wisdom that can't be harnessed in youth
Won't present a pure-dreamed perfection
Moments unequal to ancient truth
Are today's rawest bleak reflection

Peep through the slim gaps of the prison
Fathomless yawning void of regret
Inescapable narrow love vision
With those bars that were much too deep-set

Missing cracked mirror showed only one
Cobweb haze of hard truth acceptance
Searing light obscured never brightly shone
Penalty of a life's long love sentence

Why

Why didn't I stay in my space
Just myself and the cats,
Reflect long on that:
My head, that world, my place
With just myself to face

What was it made me leave
Perfect solo isolation,
Pain, desolation,
Lost love a life to grieve,
Heart dreams to disbelieve

Didn't know the time or year
Fire was in my mind,
Burnt love had made me blind,
Tried to pretend I didn't care
When you were never there

Abandoned myself then, lost
Visions seen just to forget
Tried so hard, and yet,
Too late and I knew the cost
My conscience I had crossed

Passions get buried deep
Black gulf yawning wide,
Dry place to lie and hide
Dreams I could never keep,
Then the past came back to weep

From the future could I borrow
Some time with a prayer,
To be with you, love, there,
Not overwhelmed by sorrow,
Some lost joy tomorrow?

The Planets

The planets were all badly aligned,
Heat brewed an inner blunt thirst,
Sunlight dazzled the wild dogs blind
Transient bubbles shone high then burst

Desire disguised the danger,
Basic juices a maligned blend,
Beast blinks today at a stranger
One wonders, what is a friend?

Reflection so acute and brighter
Journeys of old joy inside the mind,
Remembering a place once lighter
Not left concealed so far behind

Leave the barking blank yesterday
Remember clear that place once known:
Love's only shared - pleasure's pure play
With knowing the bliss that's spent alone

The Only Way

Walking in the lonely divide

The only way I could see

That I could continue and hide

What you had meant to me

Things unspoken, memories

And the words I couldn't say

Swept away, mist over trees

Existing the silent way

Now I hear you talk to me

My dreams for you return

All that you deserve to be

What we both can now learn

Whatever comes tomorrow

Keep your fingers crossed

That we can laugh and borrow

Back something that we lost

Passed That House

Passed that house today and
Something pulled the trigger
Memories too black, recall
Knew for you I didn't figure
Here you are again today
More alive than before
Keep trying to see me opening
Not finally closing that door
In my dreams I'm holding you
And touch your hand and mind
Wonder how I ran this far
When I was always blind
You once, a golden dream
Me, a small page in your youth
Wonder might you think now
If I somehow saw some truth

Vast, the thicket's tangled

Spirits clear with confusion

Escape but try and see

Some reality not delusion

Passed that house today

A fool once lived inside

Three years alone and

A lifetime trying to hide

Unforeseen Rocks

Think I could tell you anything:

Honesty - and what's there to lose?

But do you also wonder now

About the avenues we choose?

Know I always hated words

Like, apron, slippers, marriage,

Successfully avoided all

But unforeseen rocks trip us,

Lives can be lived together

But out of mind and tune

With armour of oblivion

And ghosts alive in the room;

Yes I held a candle then

Don't know if you caught sight?

Then it tapered down so low

And I thought how I might

Have held a torch so high for you

Gathered your dreams to mine

Distant dusty roads ago

Almost lost and almost blind,

Words bounce off some people

Like grey raindrops on a stone

So in future I'll look forward

Not think of what's now gone

Sadness cries inside for those

Secrets, buried with our youth

I could tell you everything

Know with you now it's the truth

Strange Tricks

Many years, months, hours and minutes,
So much time and so long ago
Those vanished thoughts left within it
Of that lost love I yearned to know

Turned sharply away from those times
Somehow I found another way
But such strange tricks I find life plays
Because I feel the same today

Wherever you may be right now
Wish I was right next to you there
But then I ask myself just how
And why I continue to care

Wonder will you keep to your word
Certain one day you will return
But when nothing is said or heard
Is there a lesson I should learn

And what can you still offer me

Maybe much that I never knew

But will that smile I really see

Mirage or miracle that is you

Know I Will

You don't have to send a red rose

Or tell me your reasons or why,

Just stand with me – look at the sky

See where this green winding lane goes,

Nothing to admit or deny

I love to hear what you're thinking

I don't need to ask anymore,

Bring bright coloured sparks as before

Our old soul essences linking

And kindred lost faith to restore

Tell me more fun things, make me laugh,

Your words in your special, soft voice,

Destined, un-chosen my heart's choice

Down this mystery shadow path,

Change blue spirits pink then rejoice

We can't see and say what's to be,

Relax, come share in life's leisure,

Make love thoughts endless to treasure,

Then sing me a new symphony

And know I will match your pleasure

Lost Glory

Ghost – wooden boat lying at the edge,

High toast raised laughing, a future pledge,

Broken, lost glory ebbs her bright gleam,

Adventures planned with a wide blue dream -

Old ceremony sparkled, new name,

Beckoned calm, wild or rough seas to claim

Gaping sad hole in her broken bow,

Hull thriving with sea thrift, pink froth now,

Sailing in sunset's bronzed memory,

Breeze blowing alone skims waves to sea,

Once strong spruce timbers splintered, rock-gashed,

Leaves faded voices astern, long passed

Shells tangle with kelp in the deep hull,

Shrill song screams of the orange-eyed gull,

Captain of yesterdays shattered wreck -

Grey pebbles anchor cold fast to deck,

Mists moan, heave oars by the silver moon,

Destination unclear - sailing soon

Often

Often I think of you
Like a fizz in champagne
And wonder some day if
We'll ever meet again?

It's you I'm talking with
When half asleep, I find,
A touch of a dream life
But do I cross your mind?

The hand that you held out
Kindred spirit joined near,
Music you share with me
I always love to hear

Maybe you dream too and
Hope to meet up again,
Life and separation
In this harsh world of pain

When I think of you I
Hope you are staying strong,
That somewhere in future
We can chat before long

Feel you often deeply,
Some bond of soul essence
And distant for so long,
What point in my pretence?

Garden Delights, (for Kate)

Oh Mrs Sinkins, your froth of fluttering frills

Fills me with remembrance, endless delight,

Your fragrance is perfect, my mind so thrills,

Fringed petals pure pleasure, in green-tinged white

And osmanthus – just where do you take me?

I'm lost afar in fantastical lands,

On the breeze I've travelled so joyfully

Taken up high on your redolent strands

And saying goodbye to winter's long bark

Lilac - incomparable sweet perfume,

Abundant, full flowered mauve, white or dark

Creating peace divine, dispelling gloom

Amongst the grass, flower of poetry

Pheasant's Eye, narcissus beyond compare,

Golden heart, russet-edged, timeless and free,

Delicate scent blows her gift through the air

And dainty, just hiding in broad low leaves
Lily of the valley, pretty small bells,
Soft memories return as the breeze weaves
Taking me back someplace else where I dwell

And although tiny and left in dull shade
When I catch your wonderful scent – woodruff,
Your quiet triumph is short in spring glade,
With you enough is just never enough

Daphne a gorgeous assault so welcome,
Again your glory is drifting in spring
Deep pastel pink bunches, leaves not yet come,
Warmer days now with high promise they bring

Caressing colours, scents infuse the air,
Enchanting delirious reverie,
True beauties, Azaleas, rapture to stir
Magnet of the heart and mind timelessly

Pelargoniums – vibrant zing, sizzling, hot,
You transport me back thousands of days
To my very first little garden plot,
Strange seed bank of my child's mind as it strays

And warm air wafting that deep summer sense
Travelling to places perfumed always,
Roses, inimitable glorious essence
Bathed in ancient romance brought by sun's rays

After the sprinkling shower is over
The darker ground dampened ready for birds,
Take me to bright meadows, wild red clover
And I'll wallow in the smell of the earth

Then when I go to far forest of firs
With high crest world waving needles above,
Cedar and pine will take me right back there
To lost lands inside that I dearly love

Words For a Bereaved Friend

And when you find the way out of the deep wood,

When you feel soft breezes again kiss your face,

You'll see a pink dawn and the clearing glow gold

Bring light in your heart for what's not understood,

Accept new joy with what you can never replace,

Let the life of music more magic unfold

May your tears water small seeds you can't yet see

And the sun bring bright flowers to bloom your way,

Life that can be lived with lost shadows and dreams

Help you smile and go forward, sing under your tree

Before sorrow swamped your life, turned colour grey

And tore your head and shredded heart at the seams

Look for the missing far pathway tomorrow

Remember the blessings of a true old friend,

With love recall good times you spent together,

Hear that laugh often to lift you from sorrow,

Those who cared for you dearly will want you to mend

Their endless love lives inside you, forever

Heart's Seasons

Spear of diamond sunlight thrust

In autumn – a rare pure treasure,

Tiny specks, swirling dancing dust

Moments watched in dreaming pleasure

Prism of promise shimmering rays

Rainbow colours vivid reflect

Our full, calm lovely burnished days

Before dark winter raging crept

Harsh callous cold thief of desire

Black cloak swept across sure delight

Hurled tears hiss on blazing fire

Shivering chaos cuts constant night

And spring – looking out for fresh sun

To warm again a weary mind

Sparkle on plans only begun

Heart's high-held hopes - dreams as designed

East winds piercing needles of frost

Destroying young shoots of fresh days

Harvests not reaped already lost

Savaged fragments in mind's eye maze

Summer rise full with perfumed flowers

Let precious senses flow once more

Shine light across peaceful hours

Chase lost seasons and life restore

Wish For A Friend

Wild waves will soon return you to quay side
With your soul washed fresh for another day
Bring you back to lost lands from far away,
So watch the wide sea for the turning tide
Currents gentle to calm rough torrents inside
Spark shadow rhythm once more in life's play

The planets will soon be shining, aligned
Then spirits will row you safely ashore
Tossed up and swept fathoms deep down no more,
High stars will send you their brightest new sign
A full yellow moon will warmly shine
And make the sky glow lighter as before

Green alive the firm ground beneath your feet

Will anchor your tired heart and mind again

To create then rise higher and attain,

With loving and magic feel more complete

Your heart singing joy with every new beat,

Memories gold in these times that remain

First line Index

A day fresh and beautiful 93

Alone in that big hall 94

An old village school, very small 136

And when you find the way out of the deep wood ... 192

Carthamus pink, viridian pale hue 164

Catch the water yesterday 96

Cold and frightened, I've ambushed myself 90

Crows early call from the roof ridge 91

Cycling long miles to Dublin 80

Dawn was just then emerging 158

Dazzle, shimmer peacocks 78

Did you ever glance in a mirror 154

Disease will strip down any wild delusion 114

Dormant, still and buried, underneath dead leaves 92

Doubt that you ever knew 66

Face still pressed sad at the glass 144

Fasten those bars tight round the bird 98

Fish forever swimming east 18

Fool's looking closer back from the mirror 104

Footsteps crying as you walk 110

Fountains falling playfully 124

Ghost – wooden boat lying at the edge 184

Glances through the golden glass 121

Glimmering gold sun rays 34

Here I am hostage with this naked soul 26

Hidden hopes, where did they fly to? 146

How deep are our hidden lives 24

I haven't been a saint 42

I must see the phoenix 58

I saw a distant shadow 32

I would not have ever been born 122

If you asked was I ever romantic 143

In some old world, lives ago 16

In some space just hiding there 84

In the dark, hidden secret space, ... 157

Invisible bars encircle my mind 168

Is 'Altruism' the name of my boat? 48

Is it like a diamond 37

Is yesterday's illusion 28

Just keep away from the cliff's edge 38

Lighter hearted yet sad, the day you returned 156

Linger just lightly, listen as the sun rises 62

Many years, months, hours and minutes 180

Met a minstrel boy with a smile 86

Morning, the mirage, enveloping haze 112

Murmuring birds high in the mighty oak 30

My spirit I surrendered 36

Now at the crossroads 74

Often I think of you 186

Oh Mrs Sinkins, your froth of fluttering frills 188

Only on days with a 'y' in 153

Palest light blue first fresh summer sky 52

Passed that house today and 176

Perhaps when there's perfume of roses 100

Personally 159

Pristine white canvasses 44

Said I was a priestess 76

Saw that ancient apparition 108

Saw that black, deep dismal puddle 25

Seagulls scream now every morning 82

See the sharp shards they're dusty, still lying there . 150

Several senior ladies smiled in those days 106

Snap the perfect young branch 132

So many days slipped by since we met 50

Somewhere on a silent street 47

Spear of diamond sunlight thrust 194

Surely the sinners can't be that thing 60

Tame only the safest creatures 126

The horse lifted his head on the hillside 102

The keys came across time down to me 20

The planets were all badly aligned 174

The scale, single feather sits by blackest boulder 88

The scars and the sorrow 56

The years seen to others often belie 72

There's a little place in my heart 162

Think I could tell you anything 178

Think we lay in that meadow 13

Thinking about it just now 140

Too kind and strong, for all the rest 70

Venus low, bright in the western sky 71

Walking in the lonely divide 175

Was it a sound as well as a feeling 22

When was the map turned upside down 152

When was the wild horse broken 14

Who could see a full, sure harvest 128

Why am I climbing the steep hill 64

Why did I never find the luck 116

Why didn't I stay in my space 171

Why not another moon - younger with love and light .. 55

Wild waves will soon return you to quay side 196

Will you take a walk with me 69

World of words left trapped inside ancient heart 101

Years ago I loved someone 148

Yes, I know I chose this one.............................. 105

You can drown in a desert 118

You caught my eye 130

You don't have to send a red rose 182

You found the forgotten silent seed...................... 39

You looked at the line drawings......................... 166

You said you had a bet with the devil 40

About the Poet and Artist
Pamela Blanchfield

Born in Liverpool the artist and writer
has been involved with many subjects
in both creative fields.
Her lifelong passions are cats and nature.

She has produced and published many items
including Beatles Quiz books, as well as her
highly illustrated series of fifteen ebooks
about her cats 'The Cats' Hotel'
which are currently available on Amazon.

Painting many commissions over the years
she also enjoys sewing and gardening.

This is her first collection of poetry.

Printed in Great Britain
by Amazon